Locks of Love

A Book of Encouragement

Holly Coop

Poetry has the power to uplift the spirits of those who feel weary and to alleviate the emotional pain that can arise when both the body and mind are suffering. Release the burdens that hold down your spirit, whether you are experiencing physical pain or struggling with emotional and mental challenges. Regardless of the difficulties you may be facing, allow your spirit to find rest in the hope and assurance that your future is always secured in the great mercy, love, and promise of Your Higher Power.

Locks of Love

A Book of Encouragement

Copyright © 2018/2020 Holly Coop

ISBN: 979-8-9911032-2-0

ISBN: 13-979-8-9911032-2-0

No part of this book in any way may be used or reproduced in any manner whatsoever without written permission except in the case of brief quotations embodied in critical articles or reviews.

TABLE OF CONTENTS

Hope's Bright	1
Uninvited	3
Where Do I Go from Here	6
My Coat of Jesus	7
Morning Prayer (My Coat of Jesus)	8
Water My Soul	9
A Robin's Call	10
Your Peace	11
My Anchor	12
A Gentle Rain of Tears	13
Morning Thanks	14

The Balancing Act	15
Clutter Kills	16
Memories to Keep	17
Pain-Free	18
A Seed of Doubt	19
Sunshine on My Shoulder - Makes me Joyful	20
Learning to Walk with God	22
The Roads We Choose	23
Running the Race	23
Compass	24
Misery Loves Company	25

God's Recipe	26
Alone in the Garden	28
In the Desert	29
Muddled Mess	30
Be Not Afraid	31
Yes You Can!	31
Against the Wind	32
God's Will	32
To Rise and to Give Rest is to Give Thanks	33
September's Sorrows	34
It's Raining Wind	35

Plans? Don't Plan on Them	36
A Memory Fades But a Spirit Remains	39
Teach Me Great Teacher	40
Some Things Never Change So Others Can	41
Time Well Spent	42
Seek Me	44
Your Guiding Light	46
The Truest Peace of Christ	47
Mercy This Way	48
Live in the Moment	50
Having an Excellent Day	50
On the Bones of My Knees	51

Forgiveness	52
Gently He Reminds	53
Desert Dry	54
One Single Breath of God	56
Heaven	58
Tears of Joy	59
Invisible Answers	60
Beginning Your Journey Each Day	61
Your Sweet Grace	61
In the Silence of Prayer	62
Entering In	63
Rain Storm	63

Soul Searching	64
Be Still	64
Lighten Up Your Load	65
Depression's Prayer	66
Start with a Clean Heart	67
Standing in Place	68
No Excuses No Regrets	69
In Silence, I Hear	70
Tangled Soul	72
Lead with Your Heart	74
Inside Out	75

Silence	76
Sunshine on My Shoulder	77
The News	79
Hair Today Gone Tomorrow	82
The Sculptor's Lump of Clay	83
Two Weeks Today	84
The Mourning Hours	90
Hope	92
Home	94
I Sit in the Garden	100
In Memory	103
A Closing Note	104
Additional Pieces	106 - 127

A piece of my heart to yours

The poetry that fills these pages was born from struggle- my own, experienced during various times in my life. Although the challenges I have faced have changed over the years, I have discovered that whenever trials return, these poems that once nourished my soul still uplift me, strengthen me, and remind me of what is good, true, right, and real. They truly help me find solace and comfort.

I began writing this book after my mother was diagnosed with lung cancer. No matter your current situation, whether you're dealing with an illness or the weariness that life challenges bring, I hope you find solace, comfort, and inspiration in my poetry.

Introduction

You may feel, upon opening this book, that you are in a losing battle. You may have just discovered the horrifying truth—you have cancer!

Even for those with the most optimistic attitudes, dealing with cancer is challenging, and you will likely be bombarded with a range of emotions. Undergoing treatment can be overwhelming for both the body and the mind. It's tough on you as the patient, and it affects your loved ones as well. Regardless of whether you choose to pursue treatment or not, the entire experience of facing cancer can and will be incredibly difficult on many levels.

Whatever you are experiencing on this journey, I hope that the poems I have chosen for this book will serve as a source of hope and inspiration for you and those accompanying you on this path.

Remember, YOU are never alone. Many others are fighting the same battle. I pray that everyone finds the strength to win this fight. I hope that one day, we discover effective means to eradicate this enemy—CANCER.

For now, I offer you a few words of encouragement to strengthen you throughout your fight.

God Bless ~ Holly

A Note to the Reader

Allow the Higher Power *in your life* to unlock the floodgates and saturate your heart with His undying love. To immerse your heart with His compassion, and promise, that He will never leave you.

"Locks of Love" is not really a book about hair loss but rather a book about losing fears and gaining complete trust in God's love. He knows your heart; He can unlock all that troubles you and release from your heart and mind the burdens that threaten to steal your joy. He can lock into your heart His peace and overflow your life with His unfathomable love. His mercy and grace are abundant.

You may ask, what inspired me to write this book. The answer would be, not what really but rather, who?

My mom is and always will be my constant inspiration.

After finding out she had cancer my mother was, as always, the pillar of strength for herself and her family. She was ready and determined to fight the good fight and win this war on cancer that had just struck her and those she loves. And strong she remained all through the entire first round of treatments. Then suddenly, there were strands of hair. Everywhere, strands of hair.

It began – hair loss!

She never thought it would get that far. The doctor said she probably wouldn't even lose her hair. The medicine they chose to try first, "for some," the doctor coaxed – "hair loss wasn't even an issue." Well, it turns out – it was an issue.

Now my mother is the humblest soul God has ever blessed the face of the earth with. There is not a VAIN bone in her body but even *she*, this gentle, humble woman without an ounce of vanity or ego – was affected. It bothered her!

Trying on wigs at first was going along well, but that took a drastic turn when none of the wigs were looking "good" on her. None were like her hair.

Score one for Cancer – it had gotten my strong, ready for battle, mother to begin to feel down.

Seeing how this affected my mother made me realize how much all the cancer patients that I had seen at the treatment center must be feeling.

Having many poems which I had written over the years, a great majority of which are inspirational and uplifting, I decided that putting them together was what I needed to do, a compilation of encouraging words for those in desperate need of encouragement.

And so, the task began. Having compiled some of my favorite pieces – I hope you will find peace, solace, encouragement, and hopefully a little laughter to help you get through every battle as you fight.

Be in it to win it!

Dedication

To my mom, the bravest most humble soul I know and to the many brave souls that fought the great fight and to those in the trenches now...your courage and strength is an inspiration to us all.

Hope's Bright

Life...
Stolen from us when we are submerged in depression's deadly current.

Hope ...
A life jacket God gives us.

When darkness grows thicker around us,

Hope is a distant speck of bright just barely visible to our naked eye.

It appears to be surrounded by and covered with a veil of darkness.

It's glisten hidden from our grasp.

But through the delicately woven fabric of emotions, we can see its bright persisting to shine through.

As we trudge through our darkness we frantically reach to pull away from the veil, but the fog of gloom that suffocates us keeps pushing us back, further away from Hope's shining force.

A will of perseverance that is not of our own pulls us through the debilitating thickness of our night and the veil is lifted, just enough to fill our lungs with a resuscitative gasp as if we had been drowned, our lungs now emptied of their liquid death and we are finally able to breathe in the freshness of a new day.

Faith pushes, while *Hope's* Bright pulls us through the darkest patches of our journey and *Grace* is what gives us nourishment while we are trudging through...Life.

Uninvited

When Cancer comes to call...

It takes up residency before you even know it's there

Attacking in silence catching you unaware

There it waits - often in disguise

It has nothing to lose by *feeding off* your time

When its existence is revealed – like an uninvited guest that never seems to leave

When Cancer comes to call - for its host there's rarely a reprieve

Like a captor - *in a twisted way* takes on the role of friend

From the many hours the hostage - has been *forced* to spend

It infiltrates itself into your every waking hour

Robbing you of freedom

Stealing away your power

Living with its presence makes it difficult to visualize – life, free

When you're kept downtrodden

With the world's remedies

Lacking strength it's easy to relinquish your spirit - concede defeat

But only in *prayer* should you fall upon your knees

Let hope pull you forward where faith can bring you back onto, your feet

You hate - You despise – You wish Cancer OUT of your life

But wishing doesn't seem to make it so

Only pure WILL can *force* it to go

Without your approval, you are thrust into battle

Unarmed with ammunition — but to Cancer, it doesn't matter

Locked in a physical prison feeling all alone

Sinking into depression - it becomes your home

While Cancer takes your body and claims it as its own

Science takes advantage of your breaking heart

Before you even agree - the treatments quickly start

To hopeful ears, they sing a healing song

To some degree, it works - Cancer begins to back down

But in your fear, it's left to lurk

And when you think it has finally gone

Returning with vengeance — again it comes to call

Chipping away at your spirit — it lingers day and night

Keeping you down - unable to cope

You struggle to fight — with decreasing hope

Cancer doesn't know it is not welcomed to hang around

It's unaware of the strength you have found

Believe that you CAN — kick Cancer's butt

For nothing is impossible with God

His strength, His hope, His faith, His love - Is really all you've got

Even when the light of hope has been dimmed to just a spec

It will be your guiding light

It's your newfound friend

All is possible with God

In your weakness He is strong

He will see you through the fight

When cancer comes to call

Where Do I Go From Here

Where do I go from here Lord?
Sweet God of love.
How do I pull my chin up,
and rise above?
How will I see the sunshine,
through all this rain?
How do I numb my heart,
to release it from its pain?
Where do I go from here Lord?
Sweet God of love.
When shadows loom in the distance,
to swallow up my dreams.
How do I move along bravely,
through all the hurt I have seen?
Through all that is hurting me.
Where do I go from here Lord?
Sweet God of love.
How do I pull my chin up?
How will I rise above?

My Coat of Jesus

My *Coat of Jesus* insulates me.

It keeps me warm in the cold,

and keeps me cool,

when the heat is on.

When I feel my temperature beginning to rise,

and it seems any minute I will blow,

just like a calming breeze,

it causes my anger to slow.

When cutting winds pierce through me,

and my boat is tossed to and fro,

just like a flickering firelight,

I am warmed from head to toe.

My *Coat of Jesus* truly is,

the only garment I need.

It is having God's loving arms,

forever embracing me.

Morning Prayer
My Coat of Jesus

Draw me near to you oh Lord, draw me near.
I know by growing closer to you Lord,
I will grow closer to becoming the woman you created me to be.
Draw me near to you Lord, draw me near.
So I can be - Lord, one with Thee.

Today I am going to put on my *"Coat of Jesus"*
It will keep me warm, with the kind of warmth that only He can provide.
It will protect me from the harsh elements of daily life.
It will shelter me from the pains, that hurt, frustration, and unforgiving produce.
I can bear all things with my *"Coat of Jesus"* on.
It is my armor to face the day.
I can be the person He created me to be.
I can possess the qualities which are He...
(kindness, gentleness, patience and, humility).
Without my *"Coat of Jesus"* on,
I am only me.
Alone I am nothing.
But in Christ I am complete.

Water My Soul

A plant can only grow when the soil is just right.
If the soil does not nourish the seed,
the plant will die and only weeds will prevail.
Today I will pick the *weeds* from my heart
and *water* my soul with all that is God.

A Robin's Call

The dreariness of February marches on in March, but...

I saw a Robin today which alerted my heart that Spring is on its way.
Though the gray haze of gloomy days may cause my mood to fall,
my frown is lifted by the sweet sound of robin's gentle call.

Your Peace

Calm the uneasiness that fills my heart.
Clear up the confusion in my brain.
Open my eyes to see the promise of sunshine,
during the downpours of rain.
Quiet the chatter that surrounds me.
Give hope a voice within my soul.
Let me hear the whispers of Your wisdom,
and when I do,
the reasoning to know.
Giving Your peace,
room to flow.

My Anchor

Thank you for lightening my day... with Your grace.

When my world has been extinguished of hope,

thank you for helping me to cope.

When a twirling storm of confusion leaves my brain feeling soaked,

You pull me from my drowning waters,

 into the dryness and safety of Your boat.

Your mercy and Your grace anchor me in place.

For all of this and more,

I give You thanks.

A Gentle Rain of Tears

What makes a grown woman cry?
Just about anything at any given time.

Whenever we feel weary, broken and alone,
To wash away the heartache.
Let tears flow.
To clear out the crevices where despair gets trapped,
In the darkest areas of our souls.
Like a gentle rain, our tears cleanse,
Until once again we feel whole.

Morning Thanks

My greatest moments of gratitude are found in the simplest pleasures...

In the gentle swaying breeze of the morning,
 I feel the hand of Jesus brush across my cheek.
Inhaling the sweet scent of early morning,
while thanking Him for the blessing...
that today I still exist.

The Balancing Act

Just the other day I made a statement while taxiing my children around (my new FULL-TIME job).

"When I am doing the things that make *me* happy, you guys are not and when I am doing the things that make *you guys* happy, I am not." My eldest daughter, thirteen going on thirty (since the age of three, mind you), brilliantly says...

just do a little of each.

Wow, why didn't I think of that?

The wise words that come from the mouths of babes!

Thank You, Lord, I couldn't imagine being an adult without my children teaching me how to grow!

Clutter Kills

Mind clutter narrowing the arteries of one's heart leaving no room for love to flow...

When my mind begins to narrow,
 I will empty it from all useless negative clutter,
thus, allowing for it to be fully stretched *in openness*.
With my mind then open and free,
from all negativities,
love will once again flow,
with every beat,
through the heart inside of me.

Memories to Keep

Think before you speak, asking yourself, "is that a memory I want them to keep?"

In a parent's mind *Childhood* travels by too fast.

Warm, sweet memories, in our aged minds, we *safely* keep secure, while hurtful, sad ones, with our increasing age, seem to blur.

But in the mind of a child, too often than not, the good memories become blurred, leaving bad memories holding a more prominent spot.

So before you allow your mouth to speak, know that what you say will be the message your child's *memory* will keep.

Pain-Free

I patiently await, Your elixir

The pain I suffer now is surely fleeting.

For now, is but a blink in the measure of Your time.

In the broader spectrum of existence, one's struggles are as a pebble tossed into the ocean.

Though barely able to see with the naked eye, its ripple across the water travels far and wide.

I am comforted in knowing the joy that is Your peace, will soon be mine.

A Seed of Doubt

Do not let a seed of doubt take root.

Let a cleansing tear wash it away.

Know that you will triumph with Christ, on His holy judgment day.

Sunshine on My Shoulder - *makes me joyful*

The sun was shining bright, on my face this morning

The biggest, brightest sun I've ever seen

It felt like God himself - was looking down on me

I felt anxiety lift away from my troubled mind

A calm comfort replaced it – at the perfect time

With sorrow surrounding - those I truly love

I felt reassured in the knowledge –

our lives are in the palms of the Almighty up above

Knowing the narrow eye of the needle - is the *way* we all must pass through

Trusting in Him is the only thing left to do

As once the twelve apostles sailed in His boat

On the surface of the water fearing not, "*with Jesus*, we will stay afloat"

Whatever pain you are dealing

With His touch there is compassion - there is healing

Whatever the outcome we can *rest* assured

Godspeed in *His will* the stricken **can** be cured

As I drove along my way

All I could do is pray

Boldly asking for what I longed to receive

"Heal oh Mighty Healer - Jesus won't you please?"

To my intellect, the Great Healer spoke

Filled with mercy and compassion – I heard the Voice of Hope

"Take heart, My child – rest your worries with Me."

"In My strength – cope - let your anguish be set free

On my path, I turned a corner

And as I gazed the road ahead

I knew the journey would prove hard

But the sight of clear, blue sky – from the window's view of my car

Erased the blues that had been clouding up my mind

Coloring my broken heart with dark

I felt the sun shining bright, upon my shoulders

From which *burden* was gently raised

I felt the joy of His presence -

In the warmth...and the beauty of the clear sun-shiny day

Learning to walk – with God

Like a toddler taking those first steps

I need Your constant assurance my balance will be kept.

Your will prodding me along

Your arms wide open, to catch me when I fall.

The Roads We Choose

Rough roads are never the paths *we* choose for *ourselves*.

They are simply a reality of the journey of our natural lives,

that God allows, which will lead us to the *narrow* path, where He awaits.

Running The Race

Stop looking for the finish line and start concentrating on the race!

Compass

Sometimes we take the wrong turns on our journey and quest for happiness but with prayer, hope, and God's grace even though *our* compasses seem to be turning us all around – *His* will always show us the way back to the home we truly belong.

Misery Loves Company

Some people are only happy when they are miserable.

Misery loves company.

Happy people - DON'T be the company they keep.

Do not allow yourself to be drawn into their drowning dreariness.

Practice self-defense. Protect your happiness.

God's Recipe

If I follow *God's Recipe* for my life, it will be good

In the mixed-up mess of my day,

I see the ingredients of God.

His recipe for my life will be good.

Though it may not look like much,

while my soul is being stirred,

when things have simmered down, it will be good.

He is sifting me to holiness, and sprinkling me with His grace.

Just a pinch of time from me will complete His recipe.

More flavorful my life will surely be.

My daily duties measured,

With moderation in mind,

My cup will spill over, with that pinch of extra time,

To fill my tired spirit with the zest - it so needs.

My heart will boil over with joy - so sweet.

My life will be a savory treat by *God's* secret recipe.

It will be good. It will be good - it *will* be good.

Alone in the Garden

Inspired by the profound words and wisdom of a dear friend...

Sometimes the true beauty of our souls can only be fully shown,

when we, just like the sunflower, stand in the garden alone.

It is in our quiet solitude that we find the freedom to simply be.

Alone in my little garden is where you will find the real me.

In the Desert

Again I find myself wandering in the desert.

Searching, waiting, hoping.

Seemingly abandoned.

But *You* are there.

You are in the wind that rises up and travels across the horizon whirling each grain of sand into what would appear a chaotic frenzy, is actually a well-choreographed dance.

Each grain landing in the precise spot laid out for it.

I feel as though I will starve and thirst to death, unable to move another step and there *You* are sustaining me and gently moving me along at my own pace.

In the dryness of the desert where I feel so abandoned, so alone,

It is there that *Your* great care for me, is shown.

Muddled Mess

I will look YOUR best after muddling through *my* mess

Though it may not be visible

While you're muddling through the mess

Know that all your troubles, God will work them for your best

Trust, in patience, that during the worst

Is when God in His mercy is most near

He will replace in your heart - joy, where now exists only fear

The sadness, tired eyes have seen
Is transformed into a much happier scene

An anxious heart - returned to calm serene

Once tangled in a muddled mess - God's grace has set you free

Your *mess will be* **His** *best just you wait and see*

Be Not Afraid

Being afraid just makes things that much scarier!

Fear is only our reaction to the unknown.

Once you face it, it is no longer a foe.

YES, YOU CAN!

For those with a negative tone -

I have but one thing to say when you say that you can't —

The first word in CAN'T Is CAN!

Against the Wind

If, while traveling your journey you find that your walk is against the wind... turn around!

God's Will

I do not *know* God's will...

I just pray for it!

To Rise, and to, Rest is to Give Thanks

I thank You, Lord for the breath, *You* have placed in my lungs, that I *may* live another day.

I thank You, Lord that to rise, I have the use of my arms and legs.

I thank You for my senses — of taste, of touch, of smell.

Of hearing and of seeing — I thank You, Lord, as well.

I thank You for my "being" and for all creation surrounding me.

For all has sprung forth, from Your hand.

You are the Artist. The universe is Your canvas.

What a glorious masterpiece!

My only request Lord, if I may — please keep me in *Your will* today.

When darkness befalls, when my dreams begin to call, as again in sleep I lay,

I thank You, Lord for the breath, *You* placed in my lungs, that I *have* lived another day.

September's Sorrows

Why is it the most sorrowful times in my life seem to have surprised me in September?

With the whisking in of autumn winds, a swirl of emotions comes swooping in. Like a freshly raked pile of the droppings from trees caught up in a flurry from their comfortable seats so too is my fragile psyche - when September sorrows blindside me.

Leaving me cold to bear winter's somber - alone.

It's Raining Wind

With every gush, leaves blow off the trees in a thunder.

Fall is here.

Halloween is on the way.

Soon we will be baking for Thanksgiving Day.

Before we know it, in the blink of an eye,

Santa and his reindeer will be high in the sky.

Winter brings wonderful things, hot cocoa, marshmallows, frozen ice cycle drops hanging off rooftops; a reason for moms to shop; snow crunching under feet, rain, snow, and sleet.

Winter is a time of year to snuggle up warm, watch old movies, and pop popcorn.

Sit with family in front of flickering firelight.

Yes, the coldness of winter brings warmth to a heart and goodness to life.

Enjoy your season!

Plans?
Don't Plan on Them

We have our hopes high
Perhaps beyond our reach at times.

We have our dreams
But in the unfolding of life, we see
Do not always fit into the scheme.

We have our prayers we cry aloud
Though the answers may not be as we would want.

It may be YES.

It may be NO.

Or simply, NOT QUITE YET.

Whatever the outcome of the chances we take

We should have NO regrets.

Failures are needed things

We should place them upon the mantels of our dreams.

They are proof that we are striving

And they are what mold our characters the best.

Our heart's desires, for today, may be put on hold.

But what tomorrow may bring is not for us to know.

We will rejoice someday when in our hearts we hear the whisper of a voice say

"Rest in My arms My child

In My will, you remain safe."

And so whatever life should bring, my heart will surely sing

because no matter how disappointing life can be

I am thankful just simply for ME.

Because TODAY I woke up!

My nostrils breathed in and out filling my lungs with air.

My eyes opened to see while my arms and legs moved me out of a bed.

And as I walked, I appreciated every little early morning sound

that filled my groggy head.

My voice uttered a happy sigh as I sipped from a cup of coffee, and I prepared to start a new day.

I was allotted some prayer time to spend

Before the awakening of my children, and my wonderful husband.

I asked for forgiveness, which in faith I knew had already been given.

Then I thanked Him again for allowing me another day to be among the living.

I asked that He bless all men, women and all the little children on earth.

I prayed that all mothers-to-be would choose to give their children - birth.

And for all of the soldiers who have and still serve – gratitude, gratitude, and more gratitude.

During this week of much to do with many Thanksgiving Day Plans –

I am thankful just as I am, with all that I have.

It all seems to be going

Just as planned.

Give thanks and thanks will be given.

A Memory Fades But the Spirit Remains

Creases along my smile show the path my heart has taken, mile by mile.

Hopefully, my character has kept me in step

on the road that is traveled by so few.

By the sparkle in my eye it is clearly seen

that I have had a wonderful journey — yes, it's true.

So let yourselves not be troubled, nor color your hearts with blue.

Although my mind has seemingly forgotten, my *heart* still knows and loves you!

Alzheimer's may have stolen my outer identity

And scrambled memories I once held dear

But where my soul abides there is a still small voice that cries —

"It is the same ole me inside of here!"

When the time arrives that I begin my travel "home"
Keep this thought in your mind and close to your heart
My spirit will be my own, and whole - the day that I depart.

Teach Me, Great Teacher

Teach me to be like You are

To be as kind and gentle, wise, and pure.

Teach me to love like You love.

Teach me Your truth, show me Your heart.

Help me to be as humble and as trusting as was Mary

To not know, yet to know

That all will be well that is not

Help me to master each test that passes along my way.

No matter how many times I stumble

That I always land on my knees

Lord, I pray.

Teach me to feel Your presence in the quiet of my heart.

Promise me from Your path, my walk will not depart.

Thank You for this bright new day and the chance for another — new start.

Some Things NEVER Change So that Others Can

In an uncertain world, there is always HOPE

Because there is always YOU

Jesus – Your *never*-changing love is what our *ever*-changing lives always need.

You are the constant in my ever-changing life.

Let Your love be *life*-changing for me.

Time Well Spent

We get so wrapped up in our everyday lives.

We forget what is important.

What is *real*.

What is *right*.

A moment spared seems too much to ask.

Not knowing that *that moment* may be our last.

We hold on to grudges, our hurt feelings - front and center in our thoughts.

Most times we cannot even remember why the fight is being fought.

Others were hurt too.

No one is perfect.

Not even you.

So, cherish the moment that is *here* and *now*.

Learn to forgive, some way, somehow.

Tomorrow may be too late to apologize to a friend.

For some, it is a beginning, for others the end.

With your loved ones - take advantage of precious hours, precious days.

Say those words, which you know you should say.

Kisses at the door might press your time —

but will be dearly remembered by those left behind.

Seek Me

When the world does not wish to be troubled and burdened with your trials,

Seek Me - My compassion will stretch for miles.

I will not grow weary of wiping your tears

My shoulders are strong and *open* are My ears.

They welcome your grief-stricken voice like a song.

I will not take pleasure in pointing out when you are wrong,

When I see you stumbling through life.

Instead, I will gently catch you, with My arms opened wide.

If I see in your eyes signs of great sorrow,

I will shine before them hope's flickering light,

so, they may envision a brighter tomorrow.

So, My child when the world does not wish to be bothered by your woes.

Seek comfort from the One, who already knows.

When loved one's ears tire of hearing about your trials,

Seek Me, My compassion stretches for miles.

Your Guiding Light

Let the *will of God* be your guiding light.

He will keep your path straight and right.

Your best interest is always in *His* sight.

So let the *will of God* be your guiding light.

The True-Peace is Christ

This we inherited by trait.

But we have been saved,

by His sacrifice, His mercy, His grace.

For all of which, we give to Him, all honor, all glory, all praise.

We thank Him for His gift of hope, which we *know* is real through faith.

Gratefully we wait for His promise to be revealed in His heavenly place,
when our weary eyes will reflect the beauty of *His* holy face.

Then we will be truly alive, when from our death He heals us, with His eternal life.

And we will know that true peace – *is* in Christ.

Mercy This Way

Thank you for Your mercy, Lord -
Your *true* forgiving grace.
Help me Lord to forgive others *that* very way.

To put the past in its place —
to let it *there*, forever stay.

For even though my lips speak "I forgive",
my heart is beating mute from the hurt that *remains*.

And though my *mind* begs to forget,
those memories keep showing their face.
When will *true* forgiveness be deposited - into my memory bank?

Where is the invisible gateway to freedom from the past?
Where will I find the open road that leads to a fresh start?
What is the *secret* Lord to a truly merciful heart?

If I could find my way Lord through the darkness that haunts my every move,
Make my way through the forest of thoughts
That fog every minute of my day.

If painful memories did not block from my sight
The way to Your guiding light
Perhaps my heart would finally know, what *true* forgiveness feels like.

Thank you for *Your* mercy, Lord —
Your *true*, forgiving grace.

I pray someday I too will forgive
Others *that* very way.

Live in the Moment

To live in the *past* is to not allow forgiveness into your life —the forgiveness of others as well as forgiveness of yourself.

To live in worry of the *future* is not trusting God

Living in the *present* is a gift — open it every morning with joy.

Having An Excellent Day

Enjoy your experience by embracing your excellence - and share it along the way.

On The Bones of My Knees

I feel a layer of fog in the pit of my gut.

It's heaviness casting my usually uplifted mood into a serious spiritual rut.

Beaten and caught in the devil's timely snare.

Wondering how I could have left my soul - a victim unaware.

Waiting and hoping somehow I will be freed,

I lift up my voice to a humbling plead,

while falling to safety on the bones of my knees.

Suffocating in the surroundings of a world's *moral* quicksand,

I am unable to breathe, as I desperately reach, for my Savior's open hand.

As I reach up to Him, to pull me, from depression's determined grip,

I hear from behind a sly subtle quip.

In a pleasant sounding voice, he teases me with choice, while hoping in my panic

I will trip, while trying to grab the apple Eve once bit.

From pride I cannot hide, from a world of greed, I will not be freed,

knowing now that on my own, it cannot be done,

to the waiting arms of Jesus – I will run.

Forgiveness

Transform the heart that beats within me to love as the one that beat, within You.

To forgive and love those who hurt me no matter how much I am abused.

To flood them with love, put their feelings above,

the hurt, tattered, broken ones of mine.

Continue to do this, time after time.

Give my memory the wisdom to know the one hurting is the one who hurts.

It is the tongue that spills insults that thirsts.

When the journey through this desert road I am on

is too much for my broken heart to bear,

please allow my blind eyes to focus through the fog,

to see You waiting there.

Your mercy is open to all to give and to receive.

It is the reason Your beating heart was placed in you, to bleed.

Your great sacrifice freed - *all* humanity.

Gently He Reminds

Calm my spirit, Lord.

Be gently reminding.

Prompt me to be joyous even when joy does not surround me.

Tap at my heart to be content when calamity is abounding.

When darkness looms near,

haunting my existence,

be the whisper in my ear,

that speaks – "you can go the distance."

Gently remind my tired mind that with Your help

whatever hurdle my willpower may face.

I can make the leap with the help of Your grace.

Calm my spirit, Lord.

Be gently reminding.

Under Your wings in the company of Your peace –

The noise of the world cannot find me.

Calm my spirit, Lord.

Desert Dry

Desert dry is not my just desserts
It was there I lay beaten – badly hurt
But with outstretched arms, You reached me –
pulling me safely into the river of rebirth.

Dry me off – For I have been drowning in my, desert.
Re-soak my soul with the quench of newfound faith.
Pour into my spirit Your sweet, saving grace,
so desert dry won't once again set my pace.

In dry times when my faith is in a state of spiritual hunger,
and for hope my soul thirsts-
When looking from within my glass seems empty,
while from the outside it is appearing to be full-
When I am drowning in my own emotional quicksand,
while being blinded from a world of moral fog-

It is there that I am left to wallow in depression-
where fear's forceful grip comfortably holds me with, strong arm.
There is where panic does ensue - disguised as friend, but is really there as foe.
Its presence makes me feel, while I travel aimlessly,
in my deserted desert – I am all alone.

With my only chance for escape, I reach out from my hidden place,

to the Lord to free me - from this prison that enslaves,

and there *His grace* swiftly pulls me - from depression's desert grave.

Dry me off – For I have been drowning in my, desert.

Re-soak my soul with the quench of new-found faith.

Pour into my spirit Your sweet, saving grace,

so desert dry won't once again set my pace.

One Single Breath of God

When things are at their very worst and no answers can be found - remember with one single breath - God can turn things all around.

Though we know not an answer and question why things are - trust that God's unfathomable love is never very far.

Though time may seem an eternity and days go by unchanged - our future is known by only He and our lives are in His hands.

Our destiny by Him alone has already been arranged.

Our rescue has been planned.

If we will only submit ourselves - to God's most perfect plan.

Patience My children your time is near - the prayers of the faithful are the prayers that I hear.

My love is abounding - it has no end.

My capacity to save you is more - than you can comprehend.

The waters may swallow you during fierce storms that rage.

But I am the water - I am the Earth - I am the Stars, The Sky, and The Universe.

I am the One that gave them birth.

So you think I can't save you from tragedies that occur?

You think I can't give you the strength to endure?

I am the First, The Only, The One.

I am the Father that gave you My Son.

I will be here until the end is the end.

And I will then make it all new once again.

Trust in Me children - My Love is at hand.

I am The Lord Your God and you are the heirs — to My Perfect Plan.

Heaven

Just call out to Her glorious love

And Heaven will come to your aid.

Heaven will be by your side, my dear.

Heaven will be by your side.

Just let go of your pride

And send up your cry

And Heaven will be at your side.

Give all your cares to the Lord my love.

Give all your cares to the Lord.

You'll soon see your worries just melt away —

when you have given all your cares to the Lord.

Send your concerns, on a prayer my friend and leave them at Heavens door

and all those burdens that worried you so

will worry you no more.

Tears of Joy

Let me shed tears to wash away the sadness.

Let Your light burn brightly within my heart, melting away the madness.

Let my strength and hope be renewed, showing the world gladness.

May my walk imitate the steps You took - while in the wilderness –

You walked for me.

And from the burden of sin that has comfortably nestled in –

stealing hearts once belonging to You -

Let *my* eyes cry only tears of joy for the love I have found in You –

replacing the sorrowful blood-stained tears, You shed for all - in a broken world.

Opening the floodgates of God's great mercy and the promise of a new tomorrow.

Letting tears of joy replace all tears of sorrow.

Drenching a world of stolen hearts with newfound love for You,

Saturated by Your grace ready to beat anew.

Invisible Answers

Just because I do not *see* any action coming from *Your* direction —
does not mean that *You* are not answering my prayers.
It is not for me to question - who, why or where — *but with the gift of faith* — my heart *knows* that You are there.
In *Your* perfect time, my soul will rejoice - when *Your* answers are revealed to me.
So just because I may not *see* any action coming from *Your* direction,
What my eyes *cannot* see - does not determine - what my heart *can* believe.

Beginning Your Journey Each Day

Make time in your daily journey for God and He will bless your every step

Your Sweet Grace

Let joy fill my heart.

Let Your peace flow through my veins.

Let me live each day of my life sustained by Your sweet grace.

In the Silence of Prayer

When pain becomes your partner -

It's stabbing pangs — your friend.

When the numbness that once engulfed your heart —

Now permeates throughout every limb.

At this advanced state of un-being —

When the future is sparse at best.

Suffering in the silence of prayer —

Becomes your only defense.

Entering In

No matter whether you are in a state of grace or immersed in the gravity of sin.
When you enter the house of the Lord – He only asks
That you leave your *pride* outside - while your *open heart* enters in.

Rain Storm

It is only with the pour of rains that the flower comes to bloom
Taking nourishment from the ground from where its roots are planted
So soak up your surroundings girl
Let sweet mother earth unveil, to this bitter world
The beautiful flower she has planted
within the heart of *you*

Soul Searching

Sometimes you have to *open* the can of worms.

Dig *deep* into the soil - to *find* the buried treasure.

Be Still

Be still - *and know that I am here*

Be still - *so you may draw Me near*

Be still - *so My voice can be heard*

Be still – My child - *Be still*

Lighten Up Your Own Load

It is an all or nothing mindset that permeates a tortured mind

Ultimately wreaking havoc throughout a person's life

Choosing to see black when another choice could be white

Never leaving any room for the gray area

To come, into light

With an attitude such as this, *error* cannot exist

And when the realization comes that you cannot measure up

Those simply unattainable standards

will leave an already troubled soul in a state of terror

If only you would realize that no one ever could

Live up to such strict codes as you think you should

It is that *all or nothing* mindset that cripples a soul from striving on

And every attempt to move ahead will be paralyzed from the start

Open up your mind to see some gray through the black and white

Give yourself a break to ENJOY the rest of your life

Depression's Prayer

My heart can be joy-filled

Just simply because I exist

My chest moves up and down, from air

My limbs can bend and twist

My eyes can view creation in a petal from a bud

And even when uninvited under my roof

I can appreciate the importance of a menacing little bug

All the intricately designed elements of nature

Leave my intellect in awe

How can a soul give its heart away, to depression's deadly call?

In just *this* instance I will utter the words "I can't" - and rejoice in that...

I can be joy-filled just simply because "I" exist - among the awe!

Be a receiver of Your grace – hang up on depression's deadly call.

Start with a CLEAN Heart

Clutter pulls me down

After cleaning through, my paperwork

Not only can I see

My desk's top more clearly

But a lot that has been bothering me

By waking up my troubled heart

Merely with this spring clean start

So many things now come into view

How wonderful it is what de-cluttering can do

When it takes place inside your home - *and you*

Standing in Place

Your feet cannot carry you forward

With your mind paralyzed in the past

The world around spins freely

Each moment more appreciated than the last

There *you* are waiting in the distance

Reliving in your mind the past

Afraid to let go of the hurting

Unaware that the *pain* is your excuse

For not getting on with the present

Because the past is all that is left of your youth

No Excuses No Regret

We all do the best that we can

From what we are given

By our command

Generation after generation you will see

Nobody has done any better *or worse* - than me

You get what you get

It is all up to you

To make the best of it

Don't offer excuses

While leaving behind - NO REGRET

In Silence, I Hear

Silencing "my prayer" and opening my heart to the listening...

When my prayers have become my lists of wants,
earthly desires, and *my own* definition of my needs –
it is time to silence my prayers
and to the listening – quickly heed

Who am I to tell the "All Knowing" what He already knows of me?
Who am I to strain to view the future when the future is not for me to see?

Who am I anyway –
but an infinitesimal component of this, the enormity – we call life

And even in my nothingness –
The Giver of All in His Wholeness of Heart –
With my heart, unites

In the vastness of the universe,
I may feel *my* existence an inconsequential element
in The Creator's all-encompassing plan

But to He whose hand sculpted The Whole —

important is just what I am

To the Great Architect —

When I am living *in, process* -

As the person, *He* created me to be —

I am living my optimal best and my contribution to the cosmic whole —

Is as significant as any of the rest

Silencing my prayers to the listening -

cause emotions churning in an indescribable mess

to the troubled soul - a little easier to digest

Tangled Soul

Untangle me, Lord
My soul is all in knots
It feels as though my heart has died
And in my chest, it rots

Emptiness surrounds me
A lonely I cannot bare
In a cold unfamiliar place - in a world that does not care
My mind is spinning round and round
Trying to make sense of it all
It comes at no surprise - somehow each time I open my eyes
I am faced with another brick wall
I know someday the time will come –
when I will no longer feel unraveled – undone

Untangle my heart Oh Lord
My soul is all in knots
It feels as though my heart has died
And in my chest, it rots

Inspire my intellect with solutions
To all that anguishes me
Allow my heart to be filled with joy
So once again in my chest, it beats

Lead with Your Heart

Travel your journey – keeping focus, on the passions that beat within your heart

Lose the negative – self talk

Stay the course – be resolute

While you walk the walk

Ignore those that try to lead you - with their own stifling doubt

They tend to think it is *"they"* - that **your** life is all about

Remember that the finish line is only visible after the start

You will arrive much sooner - by leading with your heart

Inside Out

Be thankful for who you know

Appreciate the gift they give

Some only see beauty with their eyes

Unable to sense one's goodness by the heart that is genuine

True friendships are denied

Too busy with the rush of life

Some pick and choose people based solely on the view

Those are the friends meant to be few

The beauty of *your* friendship

I cannot live without

Your goodness shines - inside out

Silence

It nourishes and heals
 Fostering an environment of peace

Take a little time for silence
Be awakened to your own heart's beat

Let it be your confidant while on a natures walk
Let it open your ears to hear the *inner* voice talk

Let it bring your awareness to the flowers and trees
Wildlife that fly- crawling critters at your feet

All creation big and small — some that lurk some that flee
Thriving in the silence where they are free

Let the clear air soak into your mind - flow your thoughts to a happier time
Allowing your spirit to be light

Surrounded and drenched in silence -
To experience the *peaceful* joys of life

Sun Shine on My Shoulder

Knowing the narrow eye of the needle - is the *way* we all must pass through -
Trusting in Him is the only thing left to do

As once the twelve apostles sailed in His boat
On the surface of the water fearing not — "*with Jesus* — we will stay afloat"

Whatever pain you are dealing
With His touch there is compassion - there is healing

Whatever the outcome we can *rest* assured
Godspeed in *His Will* the stricken **can** be cured

As I drove along my way
All I could do is pray

Boldly asking for what I longed to receive
"Heal oh Mighty Healer - Jesus won't you please?"

To my intellect, the Great Healer spoke
Filled with mercy and compassion — I heard the Voice of Hope

"Take heart, My child – rest your worries with Me."
"In My strength – cope - let your anguish be set free."

On my path, I turned a corner
And as I gazed the road ahead

I knew the journey would prove hard
But the sight of clear, blue sky – from the window view of my car

Erased the blues that had been clouding up my mind –
coloring my broken heart with dark

I felt the sun shining bright, upon my shoulders -
from which *burden* was gently raised

I felt the joy of His presence -
In the warmth...and the beauty of the clear sun-shiny day

The News

Dedicated to a brave woman I know and love – my mom

The exam room was silent
Not a single audible sound
Though the chattering of nerves vibrated
From the family huddled-mound

If rolling tears could be heard
The volume would have been absurd
Love for her was what kept them tightly bound
All feared the days ahead would find them, slowly becoming unwound

Anxiously they wait
In the hope to be waiting, more
Please Lord only good news concerning this woman we adore

The door hinges creaked
A bright face peeked
"The doctor will be in soon"

You could feel and hear the air from every lung, exhale deep and long

Patiently they sit

Waiting for the news

Toe-tapping ensues

Paired with unison sighs

"Why must we be kept in this state, of *doctor-waiting-room* exile?"

Again the door opens

The doctor steps inside

Her thumbs flip through papers clipped to a board

Looking up from eyewear carefully teetering from her nose

Mouth corners curl up

White teeth exposed

"Folks it's good news"

A knot in every throat — swallowed

The sound of elation followed

Ceased was the tapping of toes

From every eye, tears of relief flow

A jolt of positive energy

Replaces a stale atmosphere of worry

Together they'll continue to pray

For a cure to come in a hurry

But for now, they rejoice in the doctor's words

"Folks - it's Good News!"

Hair Today – Gone Tomorrow

Don't be self-conscience about your thinning hair

It is your heart that I see when I look at you

And I see that heart when I look into those beautiful blue eyes

And when I am blessed with the radiance of that glorious smile

And when I notice the humble kindness that you bestow on others expecting nothing in return

Hair?

What Hair?

The only thing I see is YOU!

Beautiful YOU!

The Sculptor's Lump of Clay

And all this

Heartache

Pain

Suffering

That we take on

As well as spew forth

As we do, onto others

Is all part of the Artist's plan

To chisel away the outer layers of our beings

To ultimately expose the beauties which lie within us all

Beauty, that was shadowed in this life

By residue from our fall

Now in death, our souls shine bright

As *He* intended all along

Two Weeks Ago, Today

I lost a piece of my heart today

The biggest part
Of my heart

My mom
She blew us one last kiss
Then for Home
She did depart

The brokenness I feel
Only Father Time
They say, can heal

I question
If eternity will be enough time
I can't imagine healing
From a heartbreak such as mine

I have lost someone who gave me life
And brightened each day of it
With her smile

Her devoted service to others
Was a rarity in this day
And some would even criticize
This humble role she played

But she knew every moment
It was Jesus who sipped from that cup
So she kept the coffee flowing
And her door open for everyone

She graciously devoted her whole life
In selfless service to others
With a genuine heart
Which was evident to all

Her smile lifted the saddest of hearts

Her generosity eased the burdens of many

She was the most selfless soul I ever met

She lived her own life modestly

But her giving was always in plenty

And her integrity never bent

She knew the secret to happiness

was NOT in the accumulation

Of material things

But that rather, true joy was known

To those whose richness was in giving

The more rapid a heart is emptied

When centered on the self

Her heart was brimming

Kindness was her wealth

Her talent of service to others
Was evident in all that she did
To every soul in need
Her smile gave a lift
And to all who were blessed to know her
She was a treasured gift

My life will never be the same
For all of us, it's forever changed
For she was loved so very much
So many lives her gold heart touched

And I will miss her until the day I die
Until then my heart will ache
For conversation, with my friend
Advice from her wise, comforting voice
She was by far the best mom I could have picked
Had I been given the choice

I thank you, God,

for Mom

And ask that you keep her safe

Until I am once again blessed

By her smiling face

The Mourning Hours

With some time now passed

My anguished, overwhelmed heart has deduced

Grief is not something you *get through*

Grief is a constant ache

You simply *get used to*

Time doesn't really heal all wounds

Time is just a great big band aid

That you can see right through

When memories surface through the healing salve

Of friend's love

That is applied

It's like trying to rip that band-aide off

Bringing tears that sting your eyes

And once again it's made clear

The old adage that *time* heals all wounds

Just another empty lie

Society likes to use

To ease those hearts that cry
Just another empty, lonely lie

It's all a silly farce
To keep our *mourning hours*
From plummeting forever into -
Their, dark

Hope

Sometimes hope doesn't come in the form we want

Sometimes hope comes from a completely opposite direction

And with it, the opening of doors to dreams

Bigger than we could have ever hoped for

And we find that this life, as we know it

Is so much more, than we had thought before

Even when all hope has been lost

And worries transgress into despair

Hope, though very minute to our intellect's eye

Remains there

Through a veil of pride, we often can't see

The things in this life we ought to care

So God in his infinite love

Begins the task, of stripping our egos bare

Until only our hearts remain

Though tattered, by a thread they hold on

Their vulnerabilities, slain, open to ridicule and stares

The only way to cope

Is to see in the distance

That glimmer of hope

Home

When I think of Home, I think of Mom

A cozy little house - On a quaint little street

Where a whole family grew up

Over the years some would remain - Some would leave

I think of soup - In an old butter bowl

With crackers neatly buttered - On a napkin's fold

I think of days off of school - Lying sick on the couch

With Mom cooking in the kitchen - And busy all around the house

She made our house so nice - So comfy so warm

She was always smiling and cheerful - Rarely did she scorn

When I think of Home - I think of meals prepared

On a green colored stove - *Her favorite color, for anyone who didn't know*

Breakfasts and lunches - Supper every night

And us, seated at a table - The whole family of five

Cookies would bake for every holiday - Or even just to have for a snack

And especially when dad ran out of malted milk balls, chocolate stars

Ice cream, and goodies like that

Christmas with extended family - Hearing jingles on the roof

And Santa came every year - Whether naughty or good

Store bought birthday cakes - In those days a rare treat

Now a day it's all anybody eats

Thanksgiving had to be the best - Just a relaxing day with *us*, her only guests

Waking up to the smell of turkey - She had stuffed in the wee hours

Just so that by noon - Her family could devour

She always set the table nice - With the china that she loved

Thanksgiving was the only day - She allowed it to be touched

Now that we're all grown - With the grandkids in tow

So many evenings we would visit - To watch favorite shows

Barely hearing the tele - While conversation flowed

"I'm headed to Louise's" - Would be my cue

What a blessing to have your mom living right next door to you

We would sit for hours gabbing, venting, with lots of laughing too

Always staying way too late

Oh how I am going to miss those precious hours

Now that I have run out of those precious days

At the time, not realizing, how special they were

Until now when we no longer have - *Her*

And I haven't even had time - To just sit home and cry

But the tears keep coming - Whether time allows, or not

I just wish they could bring with them - More time with my mom

When I think of Home - I think of Mom

No longer there - And my heart feels empty and bare

She left just a couple weeks ago - To tend to our *eternal* home

She will keep it cozy and warm

And fill our hearts with love

While she mothers from above

Still - I'll be forever sad

At the loss of both, my mom and dad

Though every time I enter my childhood home

I'll feel anything *but* all alone

For memories there - Surround me

A few bad but mostly all good

When I think of Home

I will always think of Mom

Who did exactly as a good mother, should

And the best any woman ever could

She lived as an angel, a saint

Patient and giving right up to the last breath she could take

With sparkling tears in her eyes

Her love for us all was shown

When I think of Mom

I'll think of an ordinary house

She lovingly made – *Our **Home***

I Sit in the Garden - Farewell

I sit in the garden surrounded by green, lush trees and flowers,
 bird's chirping in glee.

A child sits beside Me - her sparkling blue eyes are wet.
She makes not a sound - while at My feet she rests.

Through the deep thick of silence in perfect rhythm with Mine -
Our two hearts beat as one - in perfect time.

Her tiny hand reaches to gently touch my cheek.
We have a conversation though neither of us speaks.

I brush from her face - soft brown hair.
I remind her that she will always have my love and tender care.

I reach for her hand and in Mine - hers I take.
Her touch feels warm as she lifts her face, to meet Me with her gaze –

I notice in the sparkle of her eyes - a glistening reflection of Mine.
She rises to leave the garden slowly waving goodbye.

Before her figure fades into the trees - she turns once to look back at Me.
I nod to her with certainty - that all will be fine.

I know she will be returning in just a short time.
Time passes quickly and soon the child returns.

Now it is My eyes that glisten with wet - while hoping she is aware
of the promises that I've kept.

I wonder if she felt the drops of the many tears I've shed -
While watching her learn lessons - some over and over again.

I sit in the garden surrounded by green, lush trees and flowers,
birds chirping in glee.

A child sits beside Me - her sparkling blue eyes are wet.
She makes not a sound - while at My feet she rests.

Her aged hand reaches to gently touch My cheek.
We have a conversation though neither of us speaks.

I brush from her face soft hair white as snow.
I remind her that she has always had My love and tender care -
her gaze meets with Mine as she silently speaks "I know"

February 15, 1938,

an Angel was born...

                                                      ...October 5, 2017, a Saint passed on

In all the years between, a selfless life was lived. Love and devotion beyond measure were given to her family, neighbors, and friends. Everyone who met her was touched by her remarkable patience, kindness, and generosity. She was and remains a most precious soul and she is missed more than words can define. She was truly one of a kind.

In Loving Memory of Janet L. Butler

I love you mom

~ Holly

So many losses

In the next few pages, I share my heart after losing some very important people/pets in my life.

Thank you for allowing me to share with you my thoughts, feelings, and inspirations as well as memories of my beloved mother through my poetry.

Since the initial release of this book, it has been over seven years since the passing of my mom and since that day not a single day has gone by that I haven't thought of her and wished she were still here in body. Never doubting that she most definitely *is* with us in spirit. This is proven time and time again by little (and some big) synchronicities that unceasingly happen in our lives.

How much heartache is a family to take? That was the question I posed to fate. You see our family was not spared any after the passing of mom. We have continued to suffer losses due to family disappointments and upsets, and the loss of more loved ones. But we have also continued to move on despite the grief. Because that is what people do. That is what a family does. We hurt, we grieve, and we learn to live through it.

In February of two thousand nineteen we unexpectedly lost our Aunt Norma Jean (named after Marilyn Monroe). She was a gift to our family and so many people. She was my godmother, and she lived right across the street from my family and me. She was my mom's youngest sister, and she took the death of my mom hard too. Her and I spent quite a bit of time together especially after mom passed. Aunt Norma's death hit me, and all of us, extremely hard. Her wittiness will be missed, and her funny stories will continue to be told by the loved ones she shared them with.

I barely had time to catch my breath from that when out of nowhere came yet another blow to my heart.

One of my dearest friends learned his cancer had returned. He messaged me that he was going into the hospital for treatment — a few days later I read that he had passed. Devastated is an understatement to the way I felt, and I can only imagine the effect it had (and continues to have) on his family.

Life goes on and Dana would be the first one to remind me of that, so I pulled myself up out of the gloom and got on with living. Then, just three months later, another loss.

In June we lost our precious puppy girl, her name was Crystalbell. She wasn't a puppy; she was nearly 15 years old (dog years) and had been ill for quite a while. We were not surprised when her time came but we were heartbroken just the same. The loss of Crystalbell was kind of a last straw for me. I felt my spirit fading. I was beginning to lose something I thought would never fade.

My hope. I was beginning to lose hope that there was a reason, a purpose, a way to cope through this life that keeps throwing daggers to pierce my heart. I turned to the only thing that takes my muddled-up mess of thoughts, memories, regrets, guilt and just plain crappy feelings, and weaves it all into something, *hopefully,* beautiful, moving, and thought provoking — my writing.

The following pages are the result. Please enjoy. See beauty. Be moved. Let your thoughts be provoked, your spirit be inspired, and be encouraged.

Time Passes on and You're Still Gone

Green Eyes Cry

I can't believe in exactly one month from today

It will be an entire year

Since the most lovely woman ever born ~my Mom

Passed on

And it hasn't gotten any easier

When my mind's eye wanders to see her beautiful face

Memories rush in

Like a blinding ocean's wave

My eyes feel the familiar sting

Of salty tears pooling in

Keeping emotions tucked in

For the days must go on as planned

I close my eyes and breathe

Remembering my mom, and dad

Tears continue spilling out

From blinking lids

And oh how my heart aches

From the reality that is

My voice quivers with a sigh

Every time I think of you, Mom

I just can't help but cry

I know that you are happier and at peace in paradise

My heart can find some comfort knowing this

And next year yet another year will have passed

And time will keep moving on

Just like that

But to all of those you left

This truth can never ring true

Because none of us will ever get over, missing you

With every thought of her, my eyes begin to sting

From salty tears that pool

From waves of memories, that rush in

The realization just hasn't hit home

But when I see the face of Mom, in my mind's eye

I know I don't cry alone

The Longest Year

And just like that

In an instant

It was gone

But *not* gone

Is the ache of a heart laden with grief

Not gone are the many nights you forget to sleep

Not gone are the hours that pass in the motion of slow

Not gone is the longing for the baby we use to hold

Taken from us in too short of time

Not gone are the saddened hearts

That for the loss of her

Still, cry

It seems the past year flew right by
But to those who mourn
Every single minute
Lasted a lifetime

Each day another, you spend your time asking
The impossible question
Why?

Each day another you awake

To another day you must accept

She's not cuddled at your side

Each day another, your heart is pained to bid her goodbye

Because every minute since she left

You relive it in your mind

She was one of Earth's littlest angels

She was a brilliant star

So bright she could not be limited

To just a mortal life

Her eyes twinkled with happy

And hearts melted at the sight of her smile

She was surely born to be an angel

A heaven's baby meant to fly

It's the only explanation

Reasonable to broken hearts

Yes, It's been the longest year

Yet in an instant, it passed by

But the sparkle of her presence cannot be limited by time

I Weep

Words cannot fully describe
Nor are there enough to write
The way I feel

And the lump in my throat
Still far too large for me to speak
So
I will simply weep

I will simply let my eyes pooling in tears
Feel the burn
And blink away the sting
I will let my heart overflowing in blue
Feel the wringing of grief
Over the loss of you

The day's air filled with billowing echoes
From lingering hearts that grieve
Long have been the hours
Since you passed on
Though we carry on with the tasks of the day
A hovering cloud of sadness

Follows our every step

Along the way

"Let my heart feel, its grief"

"Time will heal the wound"

"She's in a better place"

All too familiar words spoken way too soon

Words that try to sugarcoat the reality

That the emptiness of loss is taking up *love's* space!

And we no longer can hold your hand, or kiss the smile upon your face

There are simply not enough sugarcoated words

To take away deaths bitter taste

Words

I too, many times have spoke

With some kind of misguided thought

We think we are helping another to cope

But the stark realization of truth

Carries a different tune

And the melody goes something like this

A heart will never complete its grief

Wounds from loss do not heal over time

The wound may develop a scab

But the scar will forever remain

Time, for the grieving

Only shifts from day to day

We move from each direction

Seeing the same reflection

In a new dimension of our emptiness

Like clockwork

We tick

We tock

Going through the motions

We are emotional robots

We travel through this new way of life

With every breath

To follow is a sigh

Over memory of your death

Honoring the goodness, of you

We're committed to doing our best

To embrace your soul's happiness

But

We never get over, loss

We simply keep moving through

Our eyes will never stop stinging

Our hearts will forever be blue

Its every beat saturated with grief

No

Words cannot fully describe

The way I feel inside

So

I will just simply

Weep

Tears Fall

October rings in sadness
For it is then
Hearts were broke
Passing times of gladness
With tears our chests are soaked
October rings in sadness
But November chimes with Hope

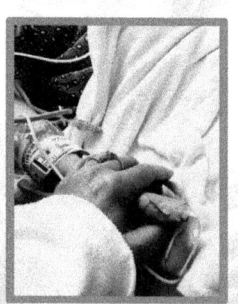

Treasures

For where your treasure is,
There, your heart will be also.
Luke 12:34

I treasure my family,
They hold the heart that beats in my chest.

This family *You* have blessed me to be a part of, from the youngest to the eldest and further yet to those who have passed beyond this earth back to You. From generation to generation, have put *their* treasure in You, as I do.
Their hearts were and are forever with You, as does my heart belong too.

My treasure Lord is in You.

After Losing You

Wearing black cause I'm feeling blue
Lost and lonely after losing you
Time will tell if I'll have strength enough
To get me through the days ahead
For they will be long and rough

Missing, crying, regretting, dying
Are just a few of the words I will use
To describe the way I am feeling after losing you

Life doesn't always prepare us
For when IT chooses to leave
But God promises we can bear it
When we choose to lean on Him and believe

The days are long
The night belongs
To my pillow, it wears my tears
Their deluge held back all day
While I must keep myself in gear

Now the moon allows me to weep
So in my pillow, I bury the grief
While crying myself to sleep

The sun will beckon a tomorrow
To usher in yet another day
That I might refresh in its newness
I know, somewhere in the heavens
For this and for me you pray

After losing you
I'll go on because you'd want me to
On the outside, I will carry on
My grief only visible to *me*
On the inside, I'll be wearing black
Because of the way I feel

After losing you

Vacation of the Heart

My heart is taking this week off
To simply wade in its sorrow
Basking in the sunshine of the day
Not troubled by uncharted waves, of tomorrow

Loss and grief are not emotions to be swept under, you see
But rather to ride with
Drifting out into the vastness of lonely
Feeling every pang
Through every degree and stage

For it is only by engulfing one's self in this feeling of sorrow
Drenching yourself in tears that after loss, surely follow
Can you arrive back on steady, dry, land
Able with hope and strength, to gain the emotional ground to firmly stand

Loss is hard
Change is scary
You ask how on earth will I get back out into the world of the living and of loving to allow vulnerability to once again peek outside of my walls?

The answer is simple
 Give it time

Take a vacation of the heart
A week off to simply wade in your sorrow

Keeping your head above the tears,
Basking in the sunshine of the day
Let your mind be saturated with memories,
Feeling with every tear you shed,
Their everlasting embrace

Gratitude

With Every Matter, Give Thanks
No Matter

When feeling
Depleted
Defeated
Despondent
With anything you are going through
If approached with a mindset of gratitude
With ease you will pass right through
Just by incorporating a few short words throughout an ordinary day
Like bless you
Thank you
Excuse me and please
You will notice a shift
A change
Your attitude will begin to align more
with gratitude

Ignite Your Life

You can't be a beacon of light in the present

If you keep letting past regrets extinguish your spark

Remember every day is a fresh start

Your future awaits

Embark

Tunnel Vision

I had to go through the dark tunnel to get to the light.

Now that I have,

I think I'll survive.

To my reader

I hope that the ending of this book does not take away your determination to

FIGHT ON!

My mom did fight, and she fought well. But ultimately, we all will face the day when it's our time to move on. The important thing is not when or even how. It's not the beginning or the end. The important thing, the ONLY thing that truly matters, IS the now. The right this minute NOW, and then the next right this minute NOW and so on and so on and so on. And spending those NOW's being kind to ourselves, those we love and those we meet along the way and spend the time we have focusing on TODAY!

God Bless and I thank you from the bottom of my heart for spending part of your journey here with me in these pages.

A little backstory...

Most if not all my poetry writing began when I was struggling through the most difficult paths of my life journey. Many times, when feeling down, troubled or just out of sorts, I will look through and re-read some of my favorite poems, the ones that were born into existence during times when I felt it most difficult to – EXIST.

I hope that those who read the inspirational pieces that I have chosen to include in this my third published work of poetry - will be blessed in some way. That you will feel a little less troubled and weary from the battle you have been forced into by no choice of your own. That you will WIN the battle and go on to live a long, happy, trouble-free life of sound mind, body, and spirit.

"Locks of Love" is a compilation of poetry to ease your troubled soul, unlock the grip that cancer has on your spirit and leave you with the hope and knowledge that your future has and forever will be locked into the great mercy, love, and promise of Your Higher Power.

Blessings to you and yours on this journey...my prayers are with you.

Enjoy more titles by Author *Holly Coop*

"A Cup of Inspiration to Go Please – My Heart Runneth Over"

"Heart Strings – Forever Wanderer"

"A Line in the Sand – A Journey Towards Forgiveness"

Available At Amazon.com

Barnes And Noble.com

HollyCoopBooks.com

Please enjoy an excerpt from my latest collection of poetry

A Line in The Sand – A Journey Towards Forgiveness

Wrecking Ball

Maybe I was part of the demolition crew,

who left rubble in your past.

But you are driving the wrecking ball,

crushing me in its path.

You are throwing the grenade,

singeing me in the blast.

You are pouring the gasoline,

and you are striking the match.

Maybe I *was* part of the demolition crew who left rubble in your past.

But you are wasting your NOW,

Limiting your future by erecting walls,

to keep me chained behind.

By holding on to your past,

you're wrecking both of our lives.

Until Next Time ~ Bless and Be Blessed

THE END

www.ingramcontent.com/pod-product-compliance
Lightning Source LLC
Chambersburg PA
CBHW050522100526
44581CB00002B/74